I0670175

"Beverly Cartwright's poetry collection, *Intact,* is a journey in search of comfort, one that seems out of reach, somewhere beyond the horizon. There is loss in this collection, and with loss comes the desire to recapture the past. Cartwright expresses that desire in several poems. "I'll have to do penance / for the times I hid your kiss, / for the times I'd like to have missed. / Keep me on your list." (Keep Me on Your List) Longing comes through strongest in I Thought I Saw You, "the illusion lasted longer than it would have without the mask. / One good thing about this pandemic, / I could maintain for ten more seconds that you were alive." Cartwright goes on to remind us that loss never leaves us, regardless of the season. "… it's too late to separate the plants out now, / The Hosta will have to stay crowded in against the orange day lilies, / Fighting with the pale Columbine I didn't plant, / the young woman who lived here before me had no children." (And It Is Spring Again) Readers will identify with Cartwright's sentiments where loss becomes a part of us. With the eponymous poem, Intact, she concludes with the truth many of us tell ourselves when dealing with loss, "a handful of delicate, white lies / that would somehow land intact, / just on the right side of our hearts." This collection is one that will hit home in the heart of any reader."

-Ken Gierke, author of *Random Riffs* and *Heron Spirit*

Intact

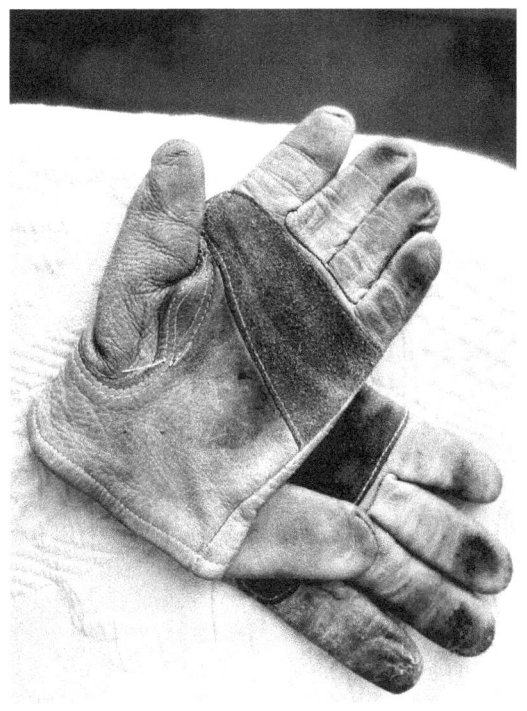

Poems by Beverly Cartwright

Luchador Press

Big Tuna, TX

Copyright © Beverly Cartwright, 2026

First Edition: 1 3 5 7 9 10 8 6 4 2

ISBN: 979-8-89975-023-6

LCCN: 2026934510

Author photo: Claire Butler

Title page image: Beverly Cartwright

Acknowledgments:

I would like to thank Susan Hankla, whose classes and workshops opened the world of writing to me years ago. I also want to thank Rick Christiansen for his unfailing support of my writing efforts. I owe a debt of gratitude to my friends and family for their encouragement, their patience, and for often being a source of inspiration.

The author would like to thank the editors of the following publications where some of these poems first appeared (in some form or another).

"For Ray:" *Oddball Magazine*
"After Hello: " *The Raven's Perch*
"The Year He Left:" *The Raven's Perch*
"Between Iron And Glass:" *Stone Poetry Quarterly*
"What Could I Say:" *Oddball Magazine*
"The Best Way:" *The Raven's Perch*
"In Blueberries:" *The Gasconade Review- No One Sees the Irony*
"In the Middle of the Cotton Trees:" *The Gasconade Review-No One Sees the Irony*
"Intact:" The Gasconade Review – *No One Sees the Irony*

Table of Contents:

Strawberry Street / 1

Home / 3

Past Her Heart / 4

Just the One Time / 5

In Blueberries / 7

In the Middle of the Cotton Trees / 9

For Ray / 10

What Could I Say / 11

Neatly Underneath / 12

The Year He Left / 15

Talk to Me / 17

The Best Way / 18

After Hello / 19

Keep Me on Your List / 21

I Was Looking / 23

I Thought I Saw You / 24

Flat Roof / 25

Elasticity / 27

We're All Going to Egypt / 29

I Fed Our Ghost Today / 30

The Madonna Hold / 33

And It is Spring Again / 34

I Climbed Inside / 35

Between Iron and Glass / 36

Brown Rice Daddy / 38

What Kind of Fire / 41

For William Carlos Williams / 42

Company / 45

Invitation / 47

If You Look Closely / 48

Berkley 1974 / 50

The Litany of Non -Movement / 52

Make Sure to Keep What You Need / 54

Intact / 56

"The past not only lives on in memory, it presses insistently upon the present."

— *Shadows on the Rock*, Willa Cather

To my mother, Eugenia Cartwright, who gave me her love of words, and the strength to write them. Her spirit continues to inspire me every day.

I.

Strawberry Street

It used to be named something non-edible,
    non-fruity,
but the city got hip for a minute and changed up
its shady interior, putting pineapples over doorways
and stained glass where there used to be rooming
    houses
with one bathroom for every four rooms rented.

No communal kitchens. It wasn't even the
    mid-sixties, it was
that ambivalent time frame before all the
    assassinations, when
everybody in their place knew damn well they were
in a place not of their choosing,
and couldn't see their way in, or out.

Who wants their landlady to have thick-soled black
    shoes
with white ankle socks and mustardy breath? My
    father doesn't.
He says a loud no in the woman's face, he doesn't
    want
his little girl seeing that every day.

Much better that she sees her mother picking up all
    the beer cans from the night before,
emptying out ashtrays, wiping down the bright,

yellow oilcloth
of the kitchen table before she goes into the only
    other room and
tries to sleep.

Tries to get five hours of peace before it starts all over
again, the walk three blocks over to the elementary
    school, holding her little
girls' hand on the way home, exclaiming over the
    latest drawing and the small clay
sculpture the teacher assured her was a baby bird,
not some nightmare she had lived through
without wings.

Home

By the time we got there,
it was a one-horse farm.
The horse himself with one
bad eye, and so old even
the youngest child could ride
alone and bareback—at least as far
as the strawberry hand house
past the rail fence,
where the rest of us waited,
crouching by the rusted hand pump.
Taking turns, open-mouthed
under the cool water,
while the horse stood grazing,
his bad eye turned to the sound
of our voices, and the good eye
watching the road home.

Past Her Heart

It seemed like she was alone in waiting for them,
leaning over the sink to pull back that linen-
    towel curtain,
the tree, the focus of her eyes, no car underneath it yet.

Across the dirt road, the sun was beginning to turn
    rosy hot
melting the already yellow cornstalks.

I always thought that cornfield was ours.
We fed the sky, didn't we?
Killing hogs, getting oily black smoke on everybody's
    hands,
even the children's.

She might have looked gentle
but the woman holding back that red-checked curtain
made soap out of lye every week,
and let me touch the live wire that kept the pigs from
getting at her garden.

"Learn you a lesson."

She told me that and I remembered then
how she looked after she washed her hair on Saturdays,
more than half of it was still black, the gray mixing in
only turning to white when it got past her heart.

Just the One Time

"When he knocked on the door I didn't open it right
    off. He looked younger
than he did the last time I saw him, right before the trip
    to the landfill, his
hair all slicked back. "Gary, ma'am. It's Gary."

"Well, anybody can see that," I told him. "I asked him
    how was Ella, and then
I asked him plain, what did he want. Don't you think I
    was right to ask him plain
Like that?" Rosa says all this over the kitchen table, our
    supper plates sitting on it
like good children ready to be excused. The tomato
slices in between the white bread slick from all the
Miracle Whip. I open my sandwich and sprinkle more
    pepper. Rosa
never uses pepper. "So what did he want?" I ask, taking
    a big bite and then a swallow of
tea. I repeat "What'd he want" because Rosa's gone
quiet, "dippy," I call it, holding her head off to the side,
like a bird that's hit the picture window.

"He wanted to know if he could borry the truck
tomorrow, seeing as how neither of us drives anymore,
'cept on Sundays. He said he'd heard there was work
over in Burgaw, and wanted to ride out there in our
truck, mind, taking the boy with him. Said they were
    both looking to work."

Rosa put her crusts down on the plate and then picked them back up for a second look. I guess she liked what she saw because she put them in her mouth and swallowed.

"You told him he could take it didn't you? Even after all that's happened." I get up and dump the rest of my sandwich in the trash.

"He said he'll bring it back with a full tank of gas. I thought just the one time" she says, her voice trailing off... "It's what Mama would have done, and George."

And to that, I can't say a thing.

In Blueberries

He came back to the farm
the summer after high school
working in blueberries every day.
A mythical job where a person's hands
take on the color of the night sky
and you can't scrub the dusk from
your fingertips, even when they idle
poised over a page, or a moonbeam
or a bead of sweat, or a stolen drop
of Old Spice.

He came back, even though he wasn't "blood"
to the uncle who paid him in damp dollar bills
that took two days to dry out, stretched flat
underneath the mattress, then hidden in a
    salvaged
legal envelope. Then hidden again in the crumbled
binding of the family bible. The bible that had
everyone's name, even his, in the same
fountain pen spidery ink.

Riding in the back of the pick-up truck
in the pre-dawn, he sat closer to the old
strawberry hands than he did to me.
He would smile at them and nod at the horizon
while he ate cold cornbread and country ham
that was more salt than anything else, more
like the taste of his mouth than anything else.

One Sunday, his real blood, a blond-haired
half brother came to visit, sitting in the front room
like a carefully placed obedience dog, waiting to
stand when the patriarch stood. Waiting for
an invitation to Sunday dinner and leaving
with nothing but a glass of iced tea.

"It was too hot to eat anyway" he told me later
as we held onto one another's waists and claimed
forever something that was more than blood.

In the Middle of the Cotton Trees

It is awkward holding you this way,
without sunlight,
without a clear trajectory

and to hear the bird's cry, its wing
a perfect fit
for your leather glove.

I pull back your arm
and line up your vision with the black bow
and the railroad tracks.

Neither of us on firm ground anymore,
even here, in the middle
of the cotton trees.

So quiet and still
moonlit teaspoons that match
the ground's pattern.

For Ray

She has the clothes that made the man.
A gray and white flannel shirt, the pocket
swollen from his eyeglass case,
A pair of Levis that got too big,
despite the new belt,
and the hand - made notch.
A clean, white T-shirt folded just so
and placed on top, left for morning
on the chair by the bed.
Nothing has been moved,
not once. Even in this month
of Sundays.

What Could I Say

It didn't surprise me at all when she
told me she had seen Jesus one morning,
crouching in the corner of the blue bedroom
just over by the dresser.

That room hadn't been blue for years
but I knew the one she meant.
There He was the answer to her prayers
and her just lying there in a thin, yellow gown
eyes closed, hoping for better days.

It must have been a delight to both of them
seeing each other like that, for she was a pretty girl
and Him, a handsome, white-bread Jesus, hair serenely
parted in the center and left to grow awhile,
like the pale hydrangea by the window.

I'd like to have seen the boy or the man myself,
all those summer nights I spent in that room,
cousins humming to sleep beside me while I declined
the pleural of agricola, agricolarum
letting the arum roll around on my tongue.

Neatly Underneath

Yesterday, I watched three butterflies circle the lilac
    bush in my garden.
They all seem to want the same flower.
Only human, I thought and I took a big, indelicate sip
    from my coffee cup.

Today, the butterflies' wings were orange dust on
    the ground,
I wanted to pretend they were still beautiful.
I wanted to take them inside and press their bodies
    onto paper
And write neatly underneath.
Always write neatly underneath when you want to
    capture death.

I learned that from my third-grade teacher,
Whose cheeks were so white and so powdery
I wanted to hold her face in my hands
And make it beautiful again.

The Year He Left

I made three meals a day
and walked the dog twice a day
sometimes on the path behind
the shed, where the pile of old
Christmas trees live.

How funny they look now,
with their branches held out
waiting for someone to notice
the unbroken, blue ornament
stuck to a lower branch,
and the paper loop from a garland
now faded to pink.

The dog has her nose down,
she has long since stopped paying
attention to the trees
and their bending ways.
I release her, letting her run
to the creek and back, while I search
for ornaments and firewood.

The return climb to the house
has us both panting, and I rush
her through the door, because
I am sure the phone is ringing,
ringing with you at the other end.

But it's a false alarm, the kind of ring
you hear from the TV in the next
room, or the neighbor who always has his
window open, even in winter.

I put the rescued ornament on this
year's tree.
I choose a center branch right in front,
I don't want to miss it again.

Talk to Me

Talk to me.
Tell me how it was,
How it used to be
How it felt to be okay back then
Rabbit tobacco lighting up
Your lungs, everybody puffing on it
Like little children trying to blow up party balloons
Red-faced with the effort
Trying to find the fun you thought you wanted.

Tell me about the nights you spent
Climbing into empty houses
To light fires and drink beer
While your brother's older friends
Talked endlessly about that Cottle girl
And her underwear that had the days
Of the week sewn on it in curvy writing
You had memorized from the Sears catalogue.

Monday was a light, pale blue that you
Thought about all week long.

The Best Way

We sat on your clean white sheet of a bed
and talked about oranges and the best way to peel
    them.

I learned a lot from watching your hands on the fruit,
but hardly any of it was the kind of thing you write
    home about,
not at twenty, or ever really.

Later, we zipped and buttoned ourselves to the
cemetery by the river and we talked about life and
    the best way to reveal it.

I listened, but by then, I had forgotten how to be both
    cold and knowing.
I just kept my eyes on yours, and my hands in my
    pockets, unpeeled.

After Hello

Listening to your voice message
I wonder what happened to the old
dial-up phone
we used to have with its holes big
enough to stick
a pen through if you are a child
wondering how things work.
Or, if you are an adult wondering why
they don't.

Listening to my own voice calling for
the dog this morning,
I didn't sound like anyone I recognized,
with or without a machine.
I called your cell and waited for my
pulse to slow,
waited for my voice to slow.

I can tell you how many syllables you
can make out of hello.
I can tell you how many blood vessels
I used to make this call.
I can tell you how the night boys
moved through my alley and
broke an old dog's back.

"Your neighborhood is beautiful" you
tell me after hello.
I dial our old house number and
imagine the ring it is making,
imagine the cicadas whirring to a stop.
The dirt floor in the garage alert
underneath its riding mower,
the house waiting
to catch its own breath before giving an
answer.

Before making sure the night light
has come on,
before making sure the moon has
come out
making the roof completely white
erasing the day.

Keep Me on Your List

Please write.
If you only forward the letter to any mailbox,
    I could find it.
I can't give you the address tonight, but I will soon.

I will have to provide postage, I'm sure.
I'll have to do penance
for the times I hid your kiss,
for the times I'd like to have missed.
Keep me on your list.

The one that you used to put out by the door at
    night.
The one with the names in bold,
in black and white.
Dead men are very popular here.

They're out every night pushing their wheels,
under the old streetlights,
under the children's new red bikes.
They push until the sparks start to fly,

And the clouds push down the sky,
and the moon begins its measured pace
and sets the night back into place.

Do you remember the way
my mouth waited with yours that Saturday?
That Delaware-street-by the river moon day,
the railroad guy with his flat tire
and our chardonnay?

Everyone misses you.
Everyone wishes you well.
Everyone is not like you remember them.

Please write.
It may be cold by the time your letter arrives.
I have a sweater for you that will fit you twice.

I Was Looking

I was looking for
something to put my faith in
And I thought about using one of the Mason
jars that my grandmother used to put up
vegetables, but I thought that might imply closure.

So, I thought about the stoneware jar
that sits in the kitchen by the microwave,
but I thought that might imply radiation
and although I am not opposed to glowing,
I don't really want to, not right now.

Then I thought, "why not put it in the white dog,
everybody puts their faith in a big, white dog,
but I took a closer look at her gum line and
decided to try something, less alive. And that's
when I remembered the green rosary with
the sterling silver cross and the sterling silver Jesus.

I thought about the summer I carried Jesus
everywhere, wrapping him around my neck,
or three times around my wrist, while I
pretended to know how to smoke
and stood too close to the boy next door.
A religious, like myself, only older with beer
on his breath and no rosary to tell.

I Thought I Saw You

I thought I saw you in the grocery store today
at least, it should have been you,
He had your height,
and that same gray hoodie,
those khaki shorts you always wore
and the real kicker,
sneakers with those socks that end before they begin
so, you have to make sure you really see them.

Even when he turned and started walking toward me
the illusion lasted longer than it would have without
    the mask.
One good thing about this pandemic,
I could maintain for ten more seconds that you were
    alive
and walking to me with that smile on your face.

It wasn't until he got within the prescribed six feet
that I stepped back a little.
His eyes were too blue to be yours
and I could see that his joy was his own
and not borrowed from Heaven the way I had hoped.

Flat Roof

We are trapped in the second-floor bedroom
After proving beyond doubt that the door to
Your room has a doorknob handle that
Sometimes misses the mark.

We are both sure one of us will
Get this thing right and the door will open.
It's a Friday night, I have laundry
and you were going to hang with friends.

I call your brother who has the extra key
But tonight, he's at a show and the phone is off.
We can't even ask a neighbor to get the one
From under a fake rock, because there is no fake rock
    yet.

And no extra key.
It starts to get late, past midnight.
You show me that the flat roof outside your windows
Is perfectly safe, so we sit for awhile
Enjoying the night sky.

Finally, I decide to call the police,
Thinking, surely, they can help.
It's beginning to feel like an emergency
To me anyway.

The police do a drive-by and slow down to shout
At us from their black and white unit.
How simple they make it- pointing to your young
    and able body-
"Climb down and break into your own house."

This is the best advice
The police can give as they ride away at 2 a.m.-
    lights not flashing

They have heard already about the desert
the soul can make out of three in the morning,
and they want no part.

Elasticity

My skin is becoming inadequate, it still covers me
but I think it has lost enthusiasm for the
job over time. Certainly, it has lost elasticity.

I am waiting for my son to leave again. He will
be back on his side of the country in two days.
    I never
want him to leave here, leave home.

It's been twenty years since the first time he flew
    across the ocean
with his fellow exchange students.
He was gone for ten months, celebrating his
    eighteenth birthday in Paris.

He missed Christmas that year. His little brother and
I ordered Chinese food and claimed a solemn
    tradition of two,
reading our fortunes aloud, while the empty chair
    looked on.

That was the first time I saw how hard
my youngest son would always work to make me
    happy, ignoring
his own growing anxiety about the world.

Later that day his dad picked him up to celebrate
    again, as though
the earlier dinner was a rehearsal for the real thing.

He hugged me once inside
and then again before he got in the car,

I remembered then what the family was like,
when we didn't have to celebrate everything twice.

We're All Going to Egypt

On Saturdays she wears his purple, felt robe,
tying the sash so tight, nobody can get
their finger behind that belt.

She deals out checks like playing cards,
occasionally murmuring
"Dear God."

God sits back with a receding hair line glued
into place, watching her take another puff
of the unfiltered Camel cigarette, a trademark,
like the robe.

He wasn't much of a talker, even then,
not like the earlier days.
He's just sitting there occasionally sipping something
    flat,
watching her add up numbers that come to same thing
every time.

"You could leave, you know."
She looks up for a minute,
and then reties the belt.

I Fed our Ghost Today

I fed our ghost today
It lives eighty-one miles south
In the back of a Starbuck's parking lot.

There's a checkerboard fence
Made from barbed wire and
Purple and white morning glories.

I placed a handful of nuts and raisins along its metal
    edge
Realizing only when my hand was empty
That I had fed what our love used to be

III

The Madonna Hold

Her shirt is pale red like the brick in the street,
and she holds the baby loosely in one arm while
I watch to see where she'll go next.

Maybe to the path by the lake where the air is cooler?
Or further down through the pine trees. I imagine the
    small
head sweating onto her forearm, slipping a little in her
    grip.

She has her own small Jesus to carry on the outside
    now.
I watch uninvited, the same way I watched the barn cat
move her kittens after I found them,
putting my human scent on their new fur.

Perhaps she'll just set him down under a tree, finding
the soft spot among the roots. The baby lifts its head
    an inch or so,
only to have gravity drop it back down as quickly as it
    rose.

I am tempted to follow her for signs of the miracle of
    this birth.
It can't have been that long ago. But she picks up the
    pace suddenly
and crosses the street leaving me alone and now afraid
    to follow.

And It is Spring Again

And it is spring again,
Something greedy this year about the hosta,
it took me too long to recognize the leaves when they
first showed up.
But then the second one crowded in and I remembered.

Today I could have told someone that you died from
an overdose.
or, I could have said "an accident."
I could have said any number of things but instead,
I just told them you got sick.

… it's too late to separate the plants out now,
The hosta will have to stay crowded in against the
orange day lilies,
Fighting with the pale Columbine I didn't plant,
the young woman who lived here before me had no
children.

I Climbed Inside

The summer he turned twenty he called himself
"John Lost John" and played the local carillon
wearing bright, orange gloves to ring the bells

He memorized passages from "The Shroud of Turin"
and quoted it to the locals outside the food co-op,

By winter, he had sold his car and hung a bike rack
from the ceiling of his kitchen.

Most of what he ate came from the dumpster behind
    the grocery store,
quarts of yogurt and sweet potatoes gone soggy.

The wood smoke from his stove made all of his clothes
smell mysterious, as though he was part of a revolution
    of one.

I climbed inside and thought well of both of us that
    year.

Between Iron and Glass

You come to the door tonight
unannounced,
unheralded.
A sudden visitor
to this new kingdom
of mine.

For a moment
as you peer at me from under your hand,
your eyes more, or less, predatory for mine.
I mistake your bulk for a wingspan
from that ancient time
when we roamed the earth together

And I mistake that mouth
for a simpler, sharper tool
a fleshy beak
ready to curve
into the evening light
and procure
its necessary food.

You tilt your head
ever so slightly
toward my iron-laced door,
requesting entry.

My own head tilts
in response.
even now,
I could show you
the preferred smoothness,
the way in.

But then where would we be?
inside here, angry birds
without even a cover
at dusk.

Brown Rice Daddy

Well I'm going up to the ashram
I'm gonna meditate on you.
Yeah, I'm going up to the ashram
I'm gonna mediate on you.
I'm going up to the ashram, honey,
Get a brand-new karmic kind of view.

Well you were my brown-rice daddy
Honey, you know you were.
Yeah, you were my brown rice daddy,
You got me into zen, zen, zen.

Well you and Richard Gere, baby,
You know you think you look alike.
Well, I got news for you daddy,
You look more like his bike.
Yeah, I got news for you daddy
He got more zen than you
Yeah, I got news for you daddy
He got zen enough for two.

Well, since you left me baby,
I been breathing on my own.
Yeah, since you left me baby,
I been chanting on the phone.
I don't think about you too much,
'cuz I'm feelin' all right.

If I thought about your vegan dish now darlin'
I jus' might lose my appetite.

Well, your astral plane is landing,
It ain't gonna land on me.
Yeah, your astral plane is landing
It ain't gonna land on me.
Yeah, your astral plane is landing,
It ain't gonna land for free.

You're gonna have a soft-landing baby,
And it ain't gonna be on me.

I heard you got a new runway
I heard it works jus' fine.
Yeah, you got a new runway
Workin' for you all the time.
You're gonna need that new runway honey,

'Cuz you sure ain't going to use mine.

Well, you told me 'bout your new baby,
Say she has good eyes,
Told me 'bout your new baby,
Said she has good eyes.
Told me she could see your aura from across the room
Yeah, she could see your big ol' aura from across the
    room,
From across a crowded room.

Well, you know to see that thing again now poppa,
She gonna need to get a zoom,
Yeah honey, to find that thing again now darlin'
She goin' to need to get a zoom,
Zoom, zoom.

What Kind of Fire

You have come here today to talk about your life, at
    least that's what it says
on the brochure: "Life Discussions" on yellow paper.
    It seems a good idea,
one worth pursuing until the woman in the red hat
    appears in front of you.

You notice the hat is pulled down too firmly on a head
    of hair that isn't there
and this feels less like a rhyme than a pair of tight braces
    on your heart that
everyone should be able to see by now, or so you think.

For yourself, you wonder when you noticed the first
    caution sign, the blink
in the eye of the child next door, or the rust on your
    favorite sweater.
It's hard to tell where a match will strike, or what kind
    of fire you'll end with.

For William Carlos Williams

Picture him
during morning rounds
students on either side
he would take the patient's hand
ostensibly to determine the heartbeat,
but more than once
he let frail hands
claim his,
let papery fingers
rest for a moment
on their journey.

He would use the proper Latin
when addressing the students,
but looking
into the patient's eyes
while they both smiled
a bit,
humoring the young,
and pondering the conundrum
of this lovely equation gone wrong
the failing body and
the strong bodied physician
each thinking of the other
each of them envious of time.

IV

Company

I am having an omelet for lunch,
egg-whites on a cast iron skillet,
it simpers without its yolk.
I slice fresh basil into green and a tomato
into red.

Lettuce, anointed with drops of olive oil and garlic
to cure the long day.
I take the first bite at the table where my sons and I
sat with their father, swallowing anger and food in
equal measure.

I can learn to eat again,
to hold my tongue in someone else's cheek.
I can learn to savor morsels,
to sink my teeth, deeper, into bigger, better bites.
I won't be ambivalent for so long at the next meal.

Eggs without the yellow, may not be the best start
     to my
new big mouth.
A little yolk would go a long way.
As I ponder whether the absence of humor really does
     indicate insanity,
smoke begins to complete the room.

Here is Anne Sexton in black on white
She wants to know if I have an ashtray in case her
    cigarette goes out.
"Not that it's likely" she smiles.

I make room for her at this family table.
I realize now,
you can use almost any wood to make an oar.

Invitation

Winter is the perfect time
to hunt for violins
the ice and snow
always attracts
a deep, red-wood finish.

The bow, too
wants to bend
through the ice
intact, tactile even
like my fingerprints
smudging over yours

I left a note for you,
I froze it right next to the
overgrown cello
and the diminutive
viola that you like to feed
in the afternoons.

It's an invitation to the very
last winter orchestral recital
behind the Home for Southern Ladies

I'll be standing outside
watching for musical instruments
at large,
loose in a field of white.

If You Look Closely

Looking around, I see a tray holding wooden beads
    and a half-burned candle, an uncapped
Chapstick and coffee from this morning.
The white Crate & Barrel vase stands nearby full of
    dried Eucalyptus, an old set of
twinkle lights are in the fireplace, waiting to be useful
    again.
A two-foot metal angel guards one side of the mantel.
She was a rescue angel; somebody's Christmas
decoration left for the dumpster the year before.
There is a scratching post for the cat and a messy bed
for the aging terrier. My sweater is still
draped across the kitchen chair from today's walk.
I should clean up—I think, then I say it aloud—for
emphasis. But instead, I look at the print
of the James River at sunset, highlighting one path
    to the island.
A photograph of my son sits in the only armchair.
    I put it away—when
people visit. But weeks go by sometimes, with him
    as my only companion.
His face is life size, his hair parted neatly and combed
    to the side. He is wearing what he called
an "interview shirt," unbuttoned at the collar in an
    attempt to relax and enjoy his birthday.
He is looking down at a present, so that you will not
    see his eyes. He is about to smile when he

looks up, but that moment went uncaptured,
  unguarded.
The glass frame broke a few years ago.
Now it is just an image on canvas. If you look
  closely, you can see—
The kiss I placed on his forehead.
Lipstick forgotten.
Son remembered.
He is where I come from.

Berkley 1974

The woman in front of me in line
 has hair that falls past her waist
 but so do all the other women here.

What made me choose her,
I don't remember. She seemed kind
or she didn't look too long at the ripped
 part of my jeans.

When I ask, the answer is yes.
She drove a light, sky blue Volkswagen
 that smelled a little like some kind of bread.
We rode most of the way in silence.

At one point, she opened a carton of juice,
 swallowed once, then handed it to me with
 an ironic tone. "I always buy what I don't need.
It's a sin really." She laughed and slowed the
car down.

We were on Contra Costa.
For a minute I was
afraid I would tell her something. I gave her
back the juice and got out with my pack.

She leaned forward.

"You okay out here?" I nodded. She drove off and waved to me from the side mirror.

I raised my hand up as the car turned and began to wave my whole arm, back and forth until it felt real again.

The Litany of Non-Movement

I'm not adjusting well, not leaving behind
what should be left, not taking a moment to gather
my thoughts—no.
I'm not forcing the issue,
but I'm not holding my breath for it either, or waiting
    while it
gathers its own momentum.
I'm not looking for the silver lining, or even for silver
    dollars,
or placing Indian Head pennies into neatly rolled
    stacks.
I'm not gravitating toward what's right
or lingering over the sunset, not waiting for dawn to
    finally arrive.
I'm not going to find out what it is that
scurries across the garage roof in the mornings.
I'm not setting any fresh traps, I'm not even trying
    to bring you
into this litany of non-movement, but I am not
    dwelling on that either.
I will not be adding the other ingredients slowly, or
    watching while
the water comes to a rolling boil.
I'm not going to sit outside
in the evening and plan the spring garden,
I'm not going to list all the names of the people
    I should thank

and post it on the front door just because so many
    of them
are no longer living, hence, no longer reading.
I'm not going to fold and refold your shirts and
    sweaters
until they have lost your scent.
I'm not going to be with you in another lifetime,
I'm not going to survey all that we had,
and I'm not going to moan my loss into the
Devil's ear, or try to make things right with
the minor gods and goddesses…

I'm not going to leave well enough alone.

Make Sure to Keep What You Need

You divest yourself of the cookbook that has gone
    brown
with age, knowing the hands that made yours once
held it new, unopened and untried.

You move the painted corner table, white and smooth,
    to the
back of the room. It is like telling a ghost hello.
You tell yourself you can say good-bye.

I imagine you sitting in a chair that is just a little
uncomfortable, one small tear on its leather arm.
You want to smoke but there is no allowing anymore
    for the follies of youth.

They used to repave Main Street every summer,
    on the hottest day
of the year, the men rolling the tar across the road
    felt their lungs
come apart by the end of the day.

I lost a ring on Strawberry Street one summer, the
    man who gave
it to me was lost from his beginning. I lost my mother
    while I looked
for silver, and china, and new cookbooks, then
    married a man I didn't want to love.

They haven't poured the new street yet, but on the
     hottest day the men will be there
inhaling tar and fumes. I will roll down the window and
     breathe with them. I will
look for rings and silver and I will want to press
     something wonderful down into
the tar, something permanent.

I'll make sure I keep what I need, and I will keep what
I thought I lost, what I have already kissed good-bye,
     what I have wiped clean
and what I opened to sticky pages.

You might think back to cigars and cigarettes
and the way we never fit together before. You and I
     have always kept
what we needed, even when no one thing or person
     remained.

Intact

After she came home from what would be one
of the last hospital stays, my mother moved
some of the furniture around in her living room
and then called me to see how I was doing, and
to see when I was planning to visit again.

Of course, ideally, I would have known about the
weekend away in room 316, but she
liked to be independent, and she liked then,
to stand in the doorway for just a few moments
striking what would have been a casual pose,
if not for the white-knuckled grip on the door frame.

When I arrive home from Alexandria, after
a two-hour drive in my 1980 Toyota, without
air conditioning, or other passengers,
I am somewhat red and somewhat flustered,
standing in the doorway of a room that has shifted,
since I last saw it, and in front of my mother
who has shifted a little as well.

She has her nurse face on, the same one she wore when
she put her hand on my forehead to check for the truth.

I could never lie to that face. I tried once,
bringing her a handful of red roses
from the next-door neighbor's yard,

telling her they had all mysteriously fallen to the ground
somehow, landing petals intact
right next to our side of the chain link fence.

She wouldn't keep them. Instead, we had to walk next
    door
and I had to give back the roses
and I had to apologize, and I had to pledge
that I would never lie to her again.

So, it surprised me quite a lot that day
when I looked at the new furniture arrangement
and I looked at my mother, and I put my lips to
her forehead to check for the truth
and I realized we were both going to tell each other
a handful of delicate, white lies
that would somehow land intact,
just on the right side of our hearts.

Beverly Cartwright is a writer living in Richmond, Va. A former medical professional who recently retired, she is now returning to an earlier love of writing. She is currently working on a second collection of poetry and a memoir about family life in the 1990's. Her work has been published in *Oddball Magazine, The Raven's Perch, Stone Poetry Quarterly,* and in the Spartan Press Anthology, *No One Sees the Irony.*

This project was made possible, in part, by generous support from the Osage Arts Community.

Osage Arts Community provides temporary time, space and support for the creation of new artistic works in a retreat format, serving creative people of all kinds — visual artists, composers, poets, fiction and nonfiction writers. Located on a 152-acre farm in an isolated rural mountainside setting in Central Missouri and bordered by ¾ of a mile of the Gasconade River, OAC provides residencies to those working alone, as well as welcoming collaborative teams, offering living space and workspace in a country environment to emerging and mid-career artists. For more information, visit us at www.osageac.org